Index

Things We Will Talk About:

Techniques, Techniques, Techniques....I want you to know what works and how to get the best results with the supplies and materials you already have or are interested in acquiring.

We will talk Basics to a certain extent, but for a full overview and introduction to Acrylic paints and products, I refer you to my first books 'Altered Surfaces' and 'Transfers and Altered Images' also published by Design Originals.

I will note which products are sewable, machine or hand washable, and which are not washable. It is important for you to know these things. I will attempt to reference 'hand' (softness of fabric) where it is appropriate. There is no real measure for 'hand' other than the way it feels or how easily it sews through fabric.

All of the techniques with fabric, canvas and paper are sewable!

Surface Basics

There are so many choices with fabrics, canvas and papers these days that it's a good idea to have some guidelines to help make decisions.

Fabrics

First, I choose to work with 100% cotton fabrics whenever I can. It is my hope that this book will serve as a resource to quilters who desire to paint or embellish their existing fabrics.

Any 100 percent cotton or blends with a synthetic work for me. Often I use white PFD (prepared for dyeing and prewashed to remove any sizing) fabric from Hoffman because it is already washed and ready to go!

Fabric comes in many weaves and it is fun to explore them all... anything from sheer voile through various weights of denim will work. Heavy unbleached muslin is also wonderful in that it introduces a totally different "natural" color to painted fabrics. If you are a collector of vintage fabrics, look for faded pieces or old linen towels.

It is always best to wash new fabrics to remove the sizing that they contain. Sizing is simply a substance that is applied to the fabric during manufacturing that keeps the fibers crisp and flat. It is not necessary to remove the sizing for art pieces or pieces you don't intend to wash.

Don't shy away from colored, or even printed, fabrics as you explore these techniques. The sales bin is a great place to look for fabrics since you are going to be changing them anyway! Fabrics can be altered with paint colors in so many different ways. You will be amazed!

Specialty Fabrics

For printed fabrics I primarily use 100% cotton. For unusual specialty fabrics I strayed into whatever was available provided it was washable. These included blends as well as 100% polyester or synthetic fibers available as wovens, lace and interfacing.

It is important to me to test the colorfastness as well as durability and washability of the paints on a variety of fabric types. I found that silk fabrics respond very well to paint applications in a unique and beautiful manner.

Quilts

I wanted to respect the washability, durability and sewability issues that quilters address in their work, so I tested the techniques first on cotton, then later on alternative fabrics.

Good quality white and natural muslin are easily available, very affordable and work very well with acrylic paints. I definitely recommend washing all fabrics to remove any sizing or residue before you add the paint colors. Personally, I work in lots of color and since I like fabric that supports any color, white seemed logical.

You can also use Hoffman PFD white cotton fabric in two weights: Lawn and Sateen. These fabrics performed beyond expectations. If you don't have a ready source for obtaining them, they are available through www.softexpressions.com.

Canvas

Any of the techniques encountered in these pages are useable not only on fabrics but also on canvas (stretched, unstretched, raw or primed) and on your favorite art papers.

I am especially fond of layering these surfaces to create mixed media pieces. Pull in some of your favorite papers, a bit of linen, some heavy muslin and create away. When you are done, put them under the machine and enjoy adding texture and details with stitching.

When working on unstretched natural canvas or heavier weight fabrics like denim I like to tear my edges rather than cutting them. I fray the edges by pulling out a few threads all around. Then I prime the center of the pieces with gesso. It gives a rustic, more primitive look to the piece. If you work with primed (already gessoed) canvas you can either cut or tear. The tears will be tighter and less rustic, but pleasing nonetheless.

Also, keep an eye out for linen canvas by the yard. It is fabulous for these techniques providing you with a tea-stained looking surface to paint on without any work on your part.

Papers

As for papers, the sky is the limit! Watercolor paper of all weights loves these techniques and sews like a dream. Rice papers can be painted and added directly to fabrics with the addition of a polymer medium. When dry, paint and stitch some more.

Notions

Consider using these techniques on ribbons, laces, trims, threads, buttons, beads and more!

Fusion Collage

As a self-taught artist, I'm used to breaking rules about materials, many times because I don't know they are there in the first place. This approach generally leads me to many combinations with many failures. That's okay by me as I learn best by discovery and don't mind trying again to work out the kinks in a formula, idea, or technique.

Combination

First of all, what is a Fusion?

In essence, a fusion is when you combine things. We know about fusions in foods. Chefs strive to combine elements of two cultures to create a new culinary style or taste.

I could say that this entire book is a fusion between fibers, papers and paint. All of the techniques I present can be done on fabric, canvas, paper or any of a number of other surfaces.

Collage

For clarity's sake in this book, Fusions refer to collage techniques that combine Fibers and Paints with something more such as Paper and Mediums (primarily Soft Gel, Polymer Medium, or Fluid Matte Medium) to create semi-flexible yet stitchable mixed-media pieces that are more like a painted canvas than fabric.

When I create a fusion I don't have to be concerned about the 'hand' of the fabric or its washability.

Mixed Media

The idea of translating techniques I use in my personal mixed media work to fabrics and papers led me to first create a Fusion. From there the rest of the techniques evolved.

Many of my students have taken their first steps into the world of fabric by creating a fusion in one of my classes. I include this section for them and for fabric artists who wish to not follow the rules!

Fusion

In a Fusion you create a base out of paper, fabric, and other notions in which numerous layers are then fused together with an Acrylic Medium. This base can be painted, sewn and embellished as you wish. You will see more later in the book.

I encourage you to try any of the techniques presented in these pages on various surfaces. If it works on fabric, it will work on paper and other interesting surfaces. A few tweaks here and there may be needed, such as a little less water or a little more paint, but you will have great fun exploring just as I did.

OPEN Acrylics

Titanium White

Alizarin Crimson Hue

Indian Yellow Hue

Sap Green Hue

Ultramarine Blue

VanDyke Brown Hue

AIRBRUSH PAINTS

Yellow Oxide

Raw Umber

Red Oxide

Napthol Red Light

Quinacridone Red

House Yellow Medium

Phthalo Green (Blue Shade)

Phthalo Blue (Green Shade)

Dioxazine Purple

Shading Gray

Titanium White

Titan Buff

Hansa Yellow Medium

Diarylide Yellow

Transparent Yellow Iron Oxide

Nickel Azo Yellow

Quinacridone Nickel Azo Gold

Transparent Red Iron

Burnt Sienna

Quinacridone Burnt Orange

Quinacridone Red Light

Quinacridone Red

Nopthol Red Light

Pyrrole Red Light

Quinacridone Magenta

Quinacridone Crimson

Yellow Oxide

Acrylic Basics
We will be working with three formulations of paints

FLUID Acrylics, AIRBRUSH Acrylics, and OPEN Acrylics. These paints come in many colors. The pigments responsible for a color have different qualities depending on their source of origin. Some pigments are shiny and sheer by nature and lend themselves to blending together to create new colors that remain shiny and sheer allowing for multiple glazes to be applied without muddiness.

My favorite colors of this type are any color with a Quinacridone or Phthalo in its name, Nickel Azo Yellow, Transparent Pyrrole Orange, Sap Green Hue, Manganese Blue Hue, Indian Yellow Hue, Dioxazine Purple, Anthraquinone Blue, Hansa Yellow….oh my, the list is really long. All these colors work great on white or light colored fabrics. Their sheerness makes them disappear on dark backgrounds.

Other colors are made up of more chunky opaque pigments which tend to cover up what they are applied over. These colors are great for blocking what is under them. Try using some of these colors on dark or black fabrics: Titanium White, Naples Yellow Hue, Titan Buff, Cobalt Teal, & Chromium Oxide Green. If you mix any of the colors from the first list with either Titanium White or Titan Buff you can create opaque pastels that will work on dark colors as well. These opaque colors also have excellent blendability with other colors, either opaque or sheer. Their opaque quality will be reflected in the newly mixed color.

The colors I have used are only partial lists of the many colors available. Visit www.goldenpaints.com for a complete listing of colors. Look for your favorites and try them.

Fluid Acrylics

Fluid Acrylics are loose, pourable, and highly pigmented colors that come in squeezable pop-top containers. They can be used as is on fabric, but will stiffen the hand.

By mixing in a special polymer called GAC 900/Fabric Medium to the Fluids you can increase the ability of the painted fabric to be laundered and help maintain its original hand. GAC 900 is also a heat-setting medium, rendering the fabrics both fully washable and dryable.

It is possible to thin Fluid Acrylics with water to create watercolor-like washes on fabrics. Adding water dilutes both the color and the density of the paint allowing the pigments to break their bond with the polymer that binds them together.

Once diluted washes are dry, they are permanent and have minimal effect on the hand of the fabric. I heat set the fabrics I paint.

Airbrush Paints

Airbrush Paints have been formulated for use in airbrush equipment. These paints are very thin and highly pigmented, making them perfect for fabrics and mixed media.

They come in both Opaque and Transparent colors.

It is important to note that these paints are not formulated for use on fabrics without the addition of either GAC 900 or the Airbrush Medium. When using the Airbrush Medium there is no need for heat-setting.

I found the fabrics treated with these paint mixtures were fully washable and dryable.

When used on paper, the airbrush paints have a consistency similar to ink. Their intense pigment load creates strong color and color washes if applied to dampened watercolor paper or canvas.

OPEN Acrylics

OPEN Acrylic paints are available through Golden Artist Colors and they are unique in so many ways. They are formulated not to skin over, to remain flexible and wet for a long period of time and have a very smooth and creamy consistency.

OPEN Paint bonds to fibers. Much to my surprise and delight, these paints became the stars of my experimentations. OPEN Paints work with two additional products: OPEN Medium and OPEN Gel.

I used both of these products at times in combination with OPEN Paints depending on the technique. All of the other Acrylic Paints and products are also compatible with the OPEN line, so there is no problem with intermixing them with the Fluids or other products you may already own.

I did not mix OPEN Paints with GAC 900, yet found the fabrics I painted to be fully washable and dryable once they had cured/dried completely.

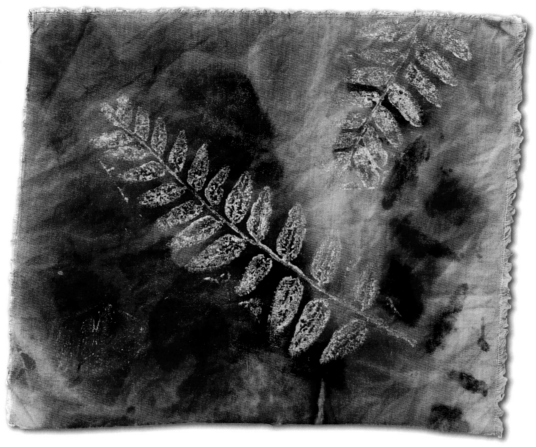

Phthalo Green (Blue)

Permanent Violet Dark

Dioxazine Purple

Anthraquinoue Blue

Ultramarine Blue

Phthalo Blue (Red Shade)

Turquoise (Phthalo)

Phthalo Green (Blue Shade)

Jenkins Green

Phthalo Green (Blue Shade)

Phthalo Green Light

Phthalo Green (Yellow Shade)

Green Gold

Raw Umber

Paynes Gray

Carbon Black

Other products that proved useful and workable with fabrics in specialized situations were Acrylic Ground for Pastels, Light Molding Paste, Molding Paste, Glass Bead Gel, and Coarse Molding Paste. I recommend hand washing and air drying any fabrics treated with these products. When thinly applied over larger areas of fabric, the fabric stiffened to an acceptable degree. It was still foldable, stitchable (using a heavy needle) and could be ironed from the back-side of the fabric using a Teflon sheet.

Applying these products through a stencil resulted in raised edges that were clearly discernible even with thin applications, similar to an embossed or flocked fabric surface.

Digital Mixed Media Grounds are another line of Acrylic Products that I used in part of this book. A full explanation of their application and usage is available at www.goldenpaints.com. In essence, they are a series of liquid coatings that can be applied to fabrics (and other surfaces) making them receptive to Ink Jet Inks and allowing you to print onto fabrics using your home printer.

They are, however, NOT WASHABLE so should only be used on decorative wall decor and quilts that will not be washed.

Gold (Fine)

Orange (Fine)

Red

Green (BS)

INTERFERENCE
Fluid Acrylic Paints

Pearl (Fine)

Silver (Fine)

Bronze (Fine)

Copper (Fine)

IRIDESCENT
Fluid Acrylic Paints

A Yard's Worth of Options

Working with Fabrics

I don't know about you, but when I walk into a fabric or quilt shop I don't usually buy white fabric. I go for the prints and patterns in lively colors that remind me of getting a new box of crayons. So my personal fabric stash has lots these kinds of patterns. I also like tone on tone fabrics with beige and cream and white patterns.

I want to share ideas with you about using Acrylics to alter colored or patterned fabrics. These also work for hand-dyes, or acrylic "dyed" fabrics.

TIP: Always look at BOTH sides of your fabrics. Sometimes the more subdued back side of the printed fabric is ideal for supporting another painted element. Especially when you pair them together!

Use Both Sides of Fabric to Create Variety

I printed a hand-cut block image of a steaming bowl of soup on both the front and back side of the same fabric to demonstrate. On the left, the image is stamped on the reverse of the fabric which reveals the pattern in a more subtle manner. When printed on the front side of the fabric the image color was strengthened to allow it to stand up to the busy pattern.

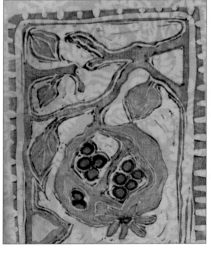  

I used a handcut block image to stamp in various colors on a tone on tone fabric. Additional line embellishments helps pull the image forward and emphasize its elements.

This traditionally hand-dyed fabric in red and yellow was embellished with turquoise color using a blend of OPEN Acrylic colors thinned down with water.

Have fun with existing patterns on fabrics, especially dyed tone on tones. Here Patt Blair chose a leaf design from a bland fabric! Even strongly patterned and colored fabrics have room for adjustment.

  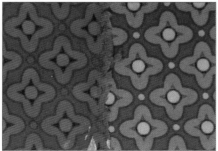

Tone on tone fabrics are great as the pattern on the fabric often resists the paint applications to create a fabric that looks totally different on the front side when compared to the back. In this image you can see that on the back of the fabric the blue paint permeated the fibers, but on the front the printed image blocked the color leaving a lighter looking fabric.

This photo shows the same tone on tone fabric with a wash of Iridescent Bronze Fluid Acrylics added to wet fabric.

An over-dye using Airbrush colors modified this piece dramatically.

In this piece, a printed fabric supports a small screen print of a plant along with several stamped images cut from erasers. The actual pattern of the fabric reads more as movement than as a separate element once the color images were applied to the surface.

TIP: Test out the color contrast of your paint choices when using patterned fabrics. Some pigments are so sheer that they really don't stand up well against a printed fabric background. This image demonstrates that the stronger green allows the bird stamp to stand out against the background print much better than the yellowish green.

It's fun to experiment with colored fabrics, print fabrics and patterns to create original color variations.

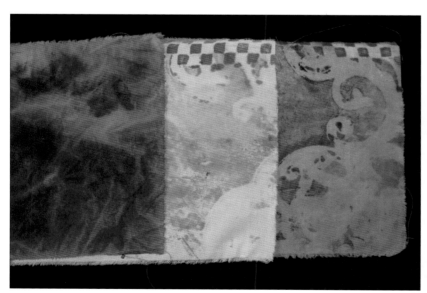

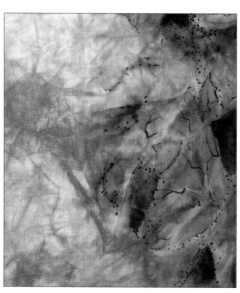

The center fabric was screen printed using various colors of OPEN acrylics. Afterwards I tore it into smaller pieces and used airbrush paints to color the screen printed fabric. You can see the original screen print colors more clearly on the orange piece, where on the purple piece the pattern is much more subtle.

This image demonstrates that the stronger green allows the bird stamp to stand out against the background print much better than the lighter yellowish green.

Starting with White for the Quilters' Delight

So Wet into Wet (13" x 13")

White muslin - mist heavily with water using a spray bottle

    1. Apply straight undiluted Airbrush Paints here and there directly from the bottle allowing them to bleed into one another naturally.

    2. Curved stripes of blue, green, brown, & burgundy added using OPEN Acrylics and water.

    3. Air dry.

    4. Heat set dry iron cotton setting.

    5. Quilted using Superior 40 wt. thread with Hobbs Poly Cotton batting and cotton backing.

"In the Cavern" (7" x 9")

Green Fabric "dyed" with Airbrush Paint and Water on white muslin

    1. Golden OPEN mixed with water and added by brush.

    2. Curved stripes of blue, green, brown, & burgundy added using OPEN Acrylics and water.

    3. Iridescent Copper Fluid Acrylics added by brush in places.

    4. Air dry.

    5. Heat set dry iron cotton setting.

    6. Quilted using Superior 40 wt. polyester threads with Hobbs cotton/poly batting and cotton backing.

I feel a certain responsibility to quilters & fiber artists to address the many applications of painted fabrics. I met a wonderful whole cloth quilter and teacher named Patt Blair who came to my studio to experiment. Patt is known for her whole cloth hand-drawn quilts that she colors with inks. Her quilts are incredibly detailed and beautifully quilted in a free form manner.

Since Patt was a painter she brings her fine art training to her quilts (www.pattsart.com). Patt jumped right in to make little tests of each of the paints on white muslin, or linen, or other "dyed" fabrics being prepared in the studio that day.

Basically, she played! As I hope you will be inspired to do. I want to begin by sharing a simplification of Patt's process. I feel confident that you will be inspired and delighted by the outcomes. When Patt brought her quilted pieces I was thrilled.

Using acrylic paints as a means of colorizing and creating pattern on fabric absolutely and positively works! Quilters can feel confident that they can create their own specialty fabrics using artist quality acrylic paints without concern for washability or permanence.

Although there will be variance to the hand ranging from almost negligible to noticeably firm, the techniques will help you choose which works best for your own projects.

Patt tried all of the paints: Fluid, Airbrush, and OPEN with equal success. Outlined below are the essential processes to get you started. You can see that Patt utilized a loose and free form painting style in her experimentations and added her own special magic when she "painted" with threads over the painted fabrics!

The addition of watered down Fluid Acrylics can change a dull fabric to a lively one in a matter of minutes. Look for opportunities to create line and pattern with your paint that are hiding the original fabric's surface.

Ethereal Waters (15.5" x 15.5")

Begin with cream colored Linen
1. Background painted by brush with Fluid Acrylic and Water mixture
2. Grid pattern (rug gripper) stamped with
a) OPEN & water mixture
b) GAC 900 and Fluid Iridescent Gold Deep mixture.
3. Allow to air dry.
4. Heat set dry iron cotton setting.
5. Quilt using Superior 40 wt. threads and 40 wt. metallic with Hobbs Poly batting and cotton backing.

Sunny Bunny (11" x 11.5")

Begin with white muslin fabric.
1. Background Painted with 50/50 mix of OPEN Medium and OPEN Acrylic.
2. Curved stripes/pattern painted by brush with OPEN Acrylic mixed with water.
3. Air dry.
4. Heat set dry iron cotton setting.
5. Quilt using Superior 40 wt. threads, Hobbs poly-cotton batting and cotton backing.

Deep-Toned Fabrics:

Creating Balance between Light and Dark

There are various products that can be used to create a white or blocked area on your fabrics. These are the ones I found most successful.

With solid or densely patterned dark fabrics, any white can help introduce much needed lightness through pattern on the surface.

You can feel the paint but it is slight. The application with the least amount of change to the hand of the fabric is the combination of the Fluid Paint with the GAC 900. It is important to note that the GAC 900 makes the white more sheer, so a second layer may be necessary for coverage. The cleanest, crispest application is with straight Fluid Titanium White, the stiffest is with Gesso.

Red Rose

Each white has a varying ability to cover a colored background. I used the whites below on this transfer over fabric to show this characteristic. When you add just a little fluid color to white before applying it to a stencil, you can create any tint you want.

Applied to any foam stamp, these whites give you more options for pattern and play on dark fabrics. These can easily be over-painted introducing either subtle or bold color to your surface.

As to the hand of white-enhanced fabrics, it is reasonable and flexible.

Titanium White
Fluid Acrylic

White Gesso

Titanium White Fluid
Acrylic with GAC 900 1:1

Titan Buff
Fluid Acrylic

Iridescent Pearl
Fluid Acrylic

White and Tinting

One of my favorite methods of introducing pattern uses a piece of rubberized rug grip grid that is available by the yard at many local fabric stores. I cut the grid into manageable pieces and use an old paintbrush to push or stipple the white paint through the open squares of the grid leaving wonderful little irregular boxes which beg for more color!

Lay rug grip material over dark fabric and stipple paint through the holes using an old brush. It is best to use a small amount of paint to avoid creating a puddle under the grid. When you lift the grid from the fabric, you can see the block pattern it leaves.

By tinting white paint with a slight amount of fluid color before applying it to the fabric, you can colorize your block pattern. The white will make the color opaque enough to block a dark background color.

Try this technique with large foam stamps or other tools.

Combine bits of colored fabrics, canvas and paper, then stitch them together for a collage journal page or wall hanging.

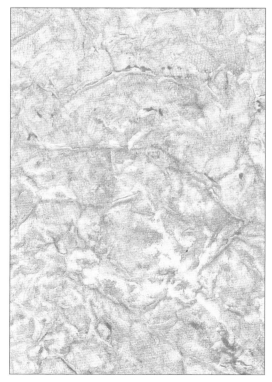

Using White Gesso

Wet fabric with white Gesso, then scrunch it into a ball. Allow to dry. Open up and pull the gessoed fabric apart after it has dried and begin to paint. Make sure to use some iridescent and interference colors with this process. The possibilities are limitless.

Sometimes it is fun to make fabric behave in a way that is unfabric-like. I often have my students ball up a piece of stiff paper, unscrunch it and then paint on it, using the ridges and valleys to capture the paint in unique ways. In my discoveries I found that if I applied Gesso to a piece of fabric and worked it into the fibers (wear gloves please) that it will stay in a ball until it dries.

Color and Deep Toned Fabrics...

Now that you've mastered the use of whites, let's return color to the areas of white by utilizing the contrast that has been created. By turning and placing stamped images on the black fabric you can create movement. Be careful to retain enough black for balance.

After painting the stamped image with additional Interference colors and stitching the surface, I added small swirls with a fine brush using a mixture of Iridescent Gold Fluid Acrylic and GAC 900. On pages 26 - 28, you can read more about fabric applications using Iridescent and Interference Fluids.

  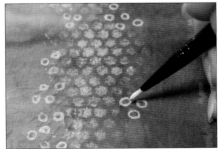

Another way to change deep toned fabrics is to use rubber stamps to create a subtle pattern over the surface. A touch of Fluid Titanium White added to any color will create a beautiful tint. Mix in a few drops of OPEN Medium and load your stamp using a sponge.

As you can see from the finished fabric, the pattern is subtle yet it enhances the dark purple/pink/green variations in the original fabric.

Try using a fine brush to "doodle" on the surface with this same mixture, or stenciling through sequin waste to give a subtle overall pattern on the surface. I used the same fabric (stamped image) and you can see how it changed the look.

Consider using texture plates with defined patterns to lay under dark fabric, brayering a light color over the surface to reveal the design.

Then paint in details to enhance the design. In this roses piece I used a foam stamp with a light application of Interference Fluid color to block areas of the black swirly fabric I wanted to work with.

Another way to change a dark solid or deep-toned overall pattern is to stencil or screen an image over the surface, essentially creating an entirely new overall pattern.

I screened this parakeet onto dark blue cotton and then "painted" it in with a variety of colors I mixed myself.

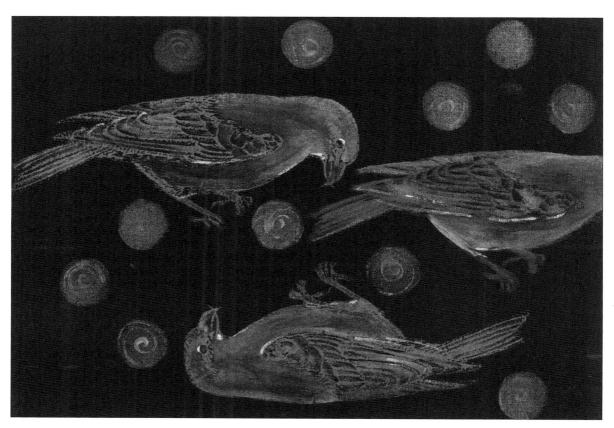

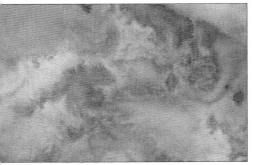
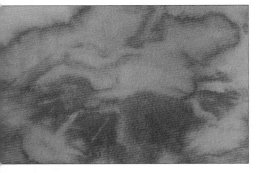
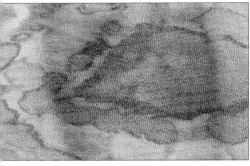

Colorizing Fabrics:
Dyeing, Tying, Dipping, Wrapping & Soaking

One of my guests during the experimental weekend in my studio was a fabulous Dyer, Anna Mae Gazo. Anna Mae is a master at creating traditionally dyed Shibori-style fabrics and she helped me work out Acrylic-based versions for some of the techniques.

Our focus was to not only colorize white fabric in a solid manner, but to hopefully create variations in the Shibori manner. I am using the word colorize here because we are not technically dyeing the fibers when we apply the paint mixtures, but painting them. The mixtures do permeate the fibers fully and in a permanent manner.

The paints of choice for this adventure are the Airbrush colors. They are already very liquid, very intensely pigmented, and mix quickly. We used either GAC 900 or Airbrush Medium along with water to dilute our mixes. There is no "exact" formula to create an individual color because color is subjective. You need to test and experiment to develop the color you desire.

The airbrush pigments are very intense; in these formulations the color takes very quickly to natural fabrics. I recommend that you practice by colorizing small swatches until you achieve the color strength you desire.

Note: WEAR GLOVES! These mixtures stain your hands.

A good rule of thumb is to add color a few drops at a time to your carrier mixture (GAC 900 or Airbrush Medium and water in a 2:1 ratio). I mix the color in glass jars with tight lids.

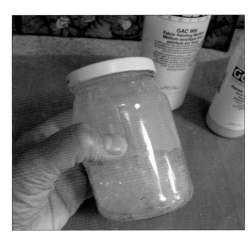

The materials needed: glass jar with a lid, GAC 900, Fluid Acrylic

Let the mixture rest until the bubbles go away.

Simple Ideas to Begin with...

1. To evenly colorize a piece of fabric, pour your prepared paint mixture into a plastic bowl or cup and push the fabric entirely under the mixture, being sure that all the fabric is submerged.

2. Wait at least 10 minutes (we waited for various amounts of time: minutes, hours, etc, but found that after 10 minutes the results were equal).

3. Remove fabric from the color mixture and allow to air dry. I put mine out on the lawn in the summer and it dried quickly. As long as the color mixture has saturated the entire piece of fabric you should have even color.

Uneven and Mottled Colors...

Should you want to create uneven or mottled color instead, this is what you do: Follow the directions above, allowing the colorized fabric to dry for only about 15 minutes (still wet but not sopping). Pick up the fabric and roll it into a ball, squeezing out any extra liquid. Run the balled up fabric under cold water briefly. Remove and squeeze again. Unwrap the fabric from its ball and lay it out to dry completely.

Once it dries you should see variations in color on the surface.

Don't forget to try colorizing patterned and previously dyed fabrics, as well as laces, ribbons and trims!

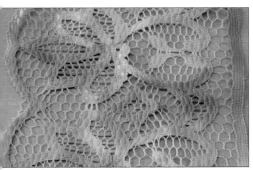

Use Bands, Clips and Clamps to Color Specific Areas...

To introduce variations in color to specific areas on fabrics, you can wrap, fold, or use rubber bands to isolate areas from the color mixture. These simple ideas can help you create lines, circles, radiating spirals, etc. If you were ever into tie-dyeing, it's time to refresh your memory.

Immersion Dyeing

This is a multi-banded piece in its orange paint bath. Note the rubber band pattern now that it has been removed from the paint bath and stretched out. Here is the piece dried and pressed. I used the rinse technique on this piece to get this mottled look for the color.

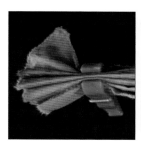  

Another formula can be created using Airbrush Medium and Fluid Acrylics. Mix 1:1 for a strong color; to soften the color use less paint and more medium.

Brush or Dip Dyeing

By fan pleating fabric pieces first, you can create a linear distribution of color on your fabric. I found that clothespins were a great help in holding my pleats while I prepared color mixtures, etc.

At times I applied the color mixture just along the edges of the pleats using a brush dipped in the color mixture. That way I was able to get linear colorations when the fabric was dry and unfolded.

At that point I could either apply the color mixture by brush, or dip the ends into one color or apply a different color to the middle.

I continued embellishing the spaces on this dyed piece with Fluid Acrylic colors mixed with GAC 900. I used a fine brush for application as I embellished the fabric with additional lines and details.

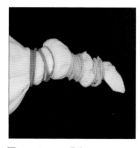  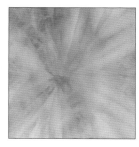

Dyeing Sheers

I used an Airbrush Medium and Fluid Acrylics mixture on a sheer piece of polyester curtain fabric. I wrapped the fabric, then I applied rubber bands or ties around a stick from my garden. I dampened the wrapped stick with water and applied the color mixture with a brush to various areas along the stick. The resulting effect was very soft and ethereal. Using wet polyester fabric as opposed to dry cotton was a factor. The polyester did not seem to accept the paint mixture as greedily as the cotton while the water diffused the intensity of the color.

Simply twist a piece of fabric and put rubber bands or ties around it to hold the twist in place. Dip the ends in color to apply paint. Apply more colors using a paint brush loaded with your prepared paint mixture. After the "dye" has been fixed by air drying, add details with other techniques demonstrated in this book.

If you want several areas that are lighter, gather up small areas and pinching them into a rubber band.

For an even distribution of color, place the rubber bands in a regular pattern on the fabric...rows of 5, then 3, then 5 again with the center row of bands placed between two of the bands in the row above.

Shibori Tying Techniques

Essentially, Shibori techniques involve pleating, folding, tying, wrapping and/or twisting fabrics to create places for color to settle and gather. By dipping, soaking, or dropping one or more colors on these manipulated fabrics, shifts and gradations of colors occur.

Using a red dye with a yellow dye should reveal gradations through various oranges. We were able to duplicate some of these shifts using our colorizing formulas. I became curious about these techniques and found that some of them are created by sewing and knotting threads in various patterns on fabrics. All that is required is a needle, sturdy thread and the ability to sew a running stitch.

Choose your base fabric. It does not need to be white or even a solid color. Prepare a needle with some sturdy thread and knot the end of your thread. Run a line of stitches somewhere on the fabric allowing space to continue sewing parallel lines of stitches for as wide and as long as you wish to colorize.

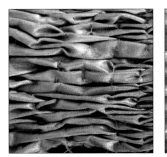 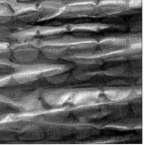

Vary your stitch size for a different look. In this example I pulled the threads with less tension to create a gathered effect. Next I applied a mixture of Silver Iridescent Fluid Acrylic with GAC 900.

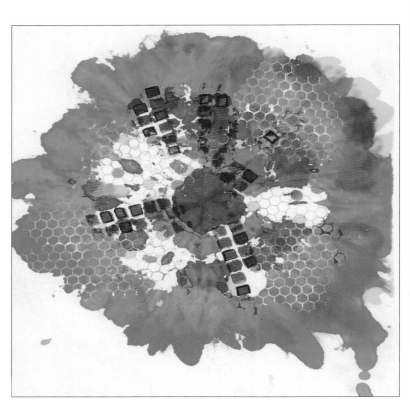

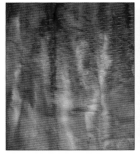  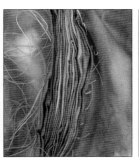  

Shibori with Gathers...

1. Each line must begin with its own thread that is knotted on the end and when you reach the end of your stitching leave a piece of thread unknotted to allow you to pull on it later. As you can see, my stitching is not straight; it will just make the outcome more random when the lines and stitches are varied. 2. Pull each thread to gather the fabric in a tight shallow pleat. The knot will hold the line in place. 3. Pull all the threads tightly by using the loose ends of thread, then knot and secure the ends tightly against the pleat 4. Paint the tops of the pleats with Gold Iridescent Fluids with GAC 900 (1:1 ratio), 2 coats. 5. After the threads are removed you can clearly see the linear markings left after the application of the paint mixture.

Shibori in Circles...

Another fun thread Shibori technique requires stitching in concentric circles! If you aren't good at imagining a circle shape, draw a chalk one onto the fabric then chalk a larger one around it. Add two or three concentric circles on your fabric of choice. You will prepare your needle with sturdy thread and a knot at one end just as in the previous technique.

 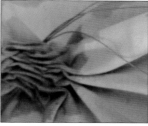

Each circle will end with a long loose piece of thread for pulling the circle up into a puff at the end. Prepare your color mixture so you can dip the puff into color! In the second image you can clearly see where the circles were dipped in a darker green - even the threads were dyed!

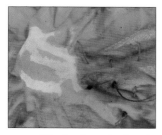 

Clip the threads after the fabric is dry and pull out the fabric to reveal a ragged donut shape. Since the colorized areas reminded me of daisies, I used my Fluid plus GAC 900 formula to add painted details to the colorized fabric.

A few more drips and drops...

1. It occurred to me that there is sometimes a need for a quick way to lightly colorize white fabric. By adding the color mixture to a spray bottle the job can be accomplished with little or no mess or fuss. It is necessary, though, to thin out your color mixture with Airbrush Extender or water so that the pigment particles don't clog the sprayer. 2. Once I had prepared this looser mixture, I put some in containers that would allow me to drop it onto the surface of fabric or onto a non-absorbent surface. This would allow me to pick the color up with a dry piece of fabric. I could lay fabric over it to pick up the color.

Spritz fabric with pale yellow mixture, then overspritz with orange. Drop green paint mixture onto surface of previously colorized wet fabric. Choose two colors and place in fine tip squeeze bottles,

Drop colors, one at a time onto areas of dry white fabric. Leave spaces of white between to avoid colors bleeding together. Lay a dry piece of white fabric over any paint residue on your craft sheet or work area. The color will be mottled and spotty. I'm sure that is all you are "dying" to know for the moment!

Waterworks!

Fabric Applications with Fluid Acrylic Paints

As a teacher, I always say, "start with what you know!" I know that when I combine Fluid Acrylics and water I am actually deconstructing the paint by loosening the bond between the polymers and the pigments.

This translates to a very different application than if I use the Fluid Acrylics with an appropriate polymer product. In the case of fabric applications those appropriate polymer products are GAC 900 or Airbrush Medium.

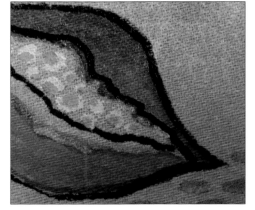

Look closely at this Pod. It demonstrates both applications. The lighter area of paint upon which the pod sits is the area I painted with water and Fluid Acrylics. It is more of a color wash, looser in style. The pod itself is painted with Fluid Acrylics and GAC 900. It shows how the GAC holds the pigments in the paint together for tighter, more even color coverage.

In this close-up of a painted daisy, you can clearly see the paint sitting on top of the fabric. It was painted without any water using Fluid Acrylics with GAC 900.

Remember...

Fluid Acrylic Paints and GAC 900 mixtures will lay an even coat of pigment over your fabrics. The colors will read clearly and not be muted or diffused.

These mixtures allow you to paint lines with sharp detail using a fine tip brush, and will leave a slightly noticeable change to the hand of the fabric you have painted. Additional layers of paint will stiffen the 'hand' of fabric.

Mix Fluids with Water...

When you mix Fluid Acrylics with water you will sacrifice the ability to create detail but will have negligible change in hand. Use this technique for diffused blends of color, softened edges, and serendipitous outcomes.

If you wish to add detail, allow your piece to dry completely and use a fine brush to introduce drawings or details with a Fluid/GAC 900 mixture.

Create Large Pieces...

You can use these techniques to create large pieces of fabric. Lay out your yardage on plastic, spritz random sections, adding your color in the manner described. Add additional colors in other sections adding more water to encourage blends and bleeds.

Repeat the process randomly over your yardage, correcting and adding color as needed.

Lois Reynolds-Mead created the yardage she used for the pages of this all fabric book in just such a manner.

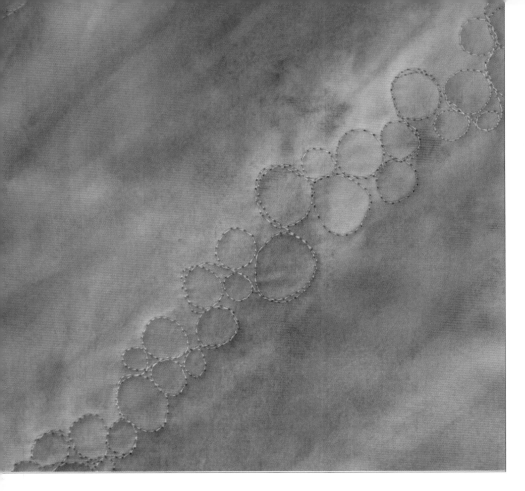

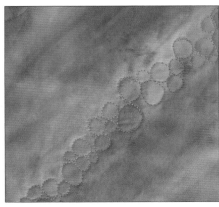

Quilted Detail...

This quilted detail of fabric that was painted using a wet brush shows that you can control both placement and directionality of your colors to an extent when working wet into wet with fabrics.

Start with a dampened piece of fabric on your workspace. Lay down bands of wet color leaving open space between each band. Begin adding clean water to the blank areas gradually connecting the stripes on either side.

The colors from these stripes will bleed into the white creating a transitional stripe that is comprised of color from both of the other stripes. Water works.

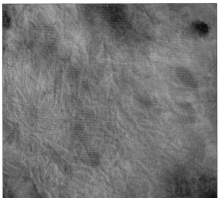

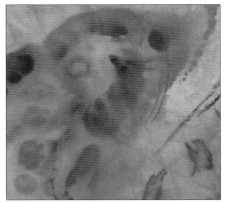

Ghost Image...

This fabric was created as a "ghost image". Sometimes there is paint remaining on the craft sheet after the original piece has been removed to dry.

You can easily capture the remaining paint to create a second piece of painted fabric. Lay a dry piece of fabric over the wet palette and allow the paint to absorb into the dry fibers. If some areas don't make contact with the wet paint, gently press the surface of the fabric onto the wet palette. Lift away and let dry.

A softer colored "ghost" fabric is the result. Recycling! This fabric was the ghost from Patt Blair's quilt entitled "Wet into Wet". How apt!!

Quilted Leaf...

In this leaf, the wet into wet technique was tweaked to allow a form to be captured. Color was laid down on dry fabric in the general shape of the leaf with a wet brush loaded with watered down Fluid Acrylics.

By first applying wet paint to the dry fabric, the darker colors were kept isolated and didn't bleed out into the surrounding fibers. I placed the lighter colors in the same manner, leaving an open space between the lighter and darker colors.

To merge the dark with the light, I used a brush with only water to gradually pull the colors towards one starting at the light side. This caused the lighter color to travel through the fibers and meet the dark color without too much disturbance along the edge. The merger appears very subtle and is easily managed by the stitch line.

Spritz with Water...

To create this effect, start with dry fabric. Stroke on the color with a wet brush loaded with Fluids Acrylics. Leave unpainted spaces around your colors.

Right away spritz water onto the areas of paint and let them start running and bleeding into each other for a vibrant but soft-edged look.

By using a fine mist spray bottle you can avoid over-spraying water into areas where you want to keep a crisp sharp line of color.

Practice this technique. The outcome is always a beautiful surprise.

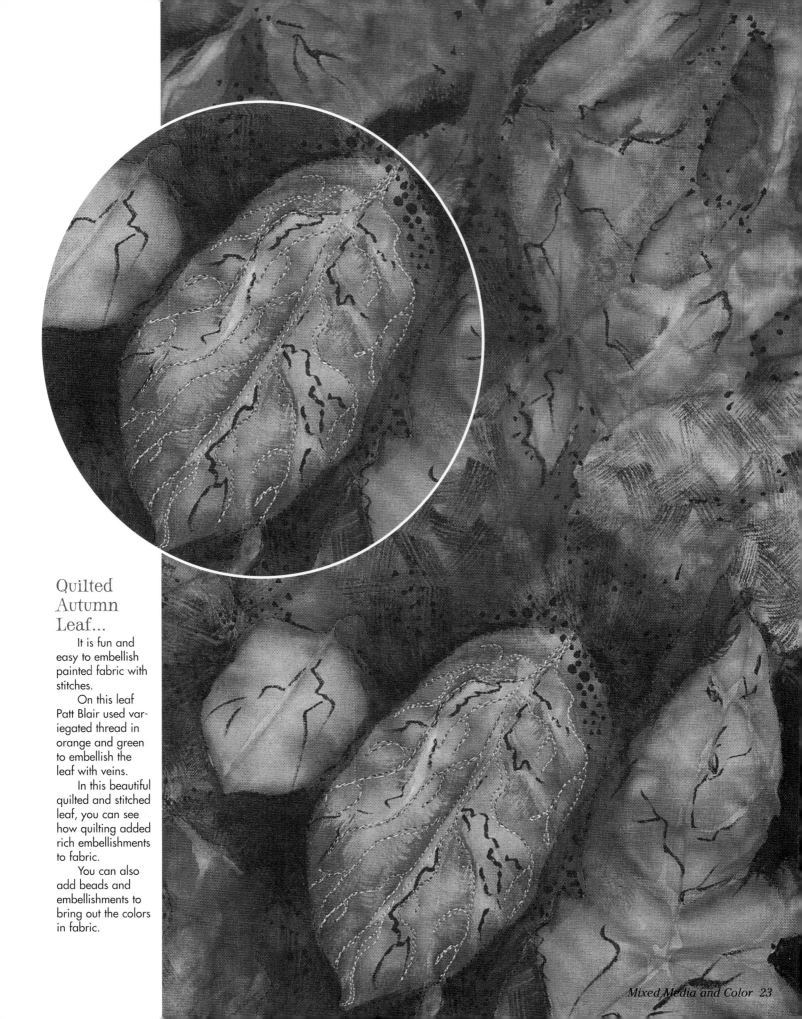

Quilted Autumn Leaf...

It is fun and easy to embellish painted fabric with stitches.

On this leaf Patt Blair used variegated thread in orange and green to embellish the leaf with veins.

In this beautiful quilted and stitched leaf, you can see how quilting added rich embellishments to fabric.

You can also add beads and embellishments to bring out the colors in fabric.

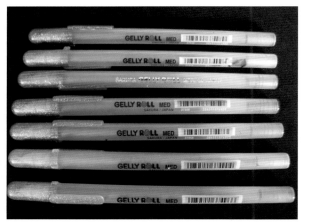

Zippity Doodle:
Writing & Marking on Painted Fabrics

We have all succumbed at some point in our lives to writing on jeans, a jacket, or some other piece of clothing. It's compelling to make your mark. Fabric is an ideal surface provided you utilize the right tools.

Sakura Gel Pens

Sakura Gel Pens work well on Acrylic painted surfaces, so I wanted to determine if this would be true on fabrics that had been coated or treated in some way with Acrylic paints or products.

To begin the test, I used the Sakura Gel pens to enhance an existing design on a piece of cotton fabric. I also added some painted areas using the Fluid /GAC 900 mixture. After the paint was dry I added additional lines with the Sakura pens. I washed the fabric by hand, and then it went into the machine to be washed again and dried. The Sakura pens worked great on fabric alone and over-painted fabric as well.

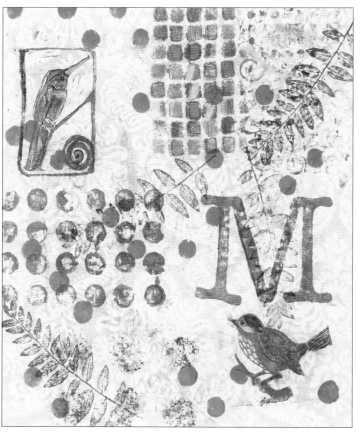

So what to try next? I began doodling on fabrics colorized with Acrylic mixtures. I stenciled some pink squares onto fabric with my rug grip pad using some Acrylic paint and proceeded to make marks around and over and on top of and through them.

I moved on to a hand-cut stamp which I doodled over and around. I tried doodling on some colorized fabrics to which I had added areas of Iridescent Fluid & GAC 900.

I switched over to Faber-Castell Pitt Artist Pens to try writing and drawing fine lines Pitt pens work well for fine line writing and drawing.

Colored Pencils

Colored pencils were next (the ones that are non water soluble).

Would they work on fabrics with Acrylic added to the surface?

I painted a light layer of gesso over a printed piece of light brown fabric and let it dry. I then colored in areas with color pencils. It showed up well and held up through handling.

I transferred an image onto the fabric and added color pencil markings to that surface. The color pencil markings went on smoothly and evenly, but were prone to smudging.

I next added a sheer coat of Acrylic Ground for Pastels (this product has a slight surface "tooth" or grit when it dries) to the fabric surface and allowed it to dry thoroughly. This gave the printed fabric a slightly faded look due to the cloudy nature of this product when it dries. The pencil marks really gripped the surface with good color and easy line formation.

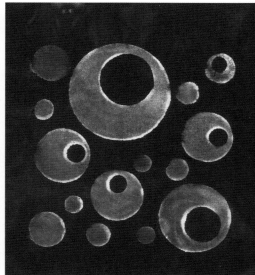

Water Soluble Colored Pencils

My set of water soluble colored pencils which give 'ink-like' results when wet are called Inktense. I wanted to try these on fabrics.

These pencils are applied either by dipping the tip into water, or painting the dry pencil marks with water afterwards. The great thing is that after they are wet, they become permanent enough to wash by hand or in a gentle cycle on warm water in the machine! By adjusting the amount of pressure you apply to the Inktense pencil, you can create color gradations on your surface. This fabric has been washed, dried, and ironed with no loss of color.

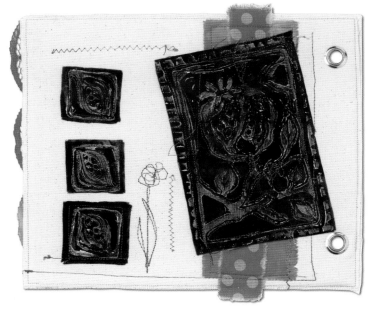

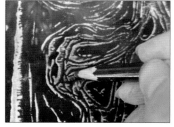

1. Select your color of pencil and dip the end into clean water to wet it. 2. I had previously inked some hand-cut stamps with gesso and stamped the images onto dark colored fabric for a test. I applied my wet pencil to the areas and started to add color. 3. Continue adding colors as desired. 4. I've stitched my color-penciled images to a page in a fabric scrapbook made by my colleague Donna Downey! Thanks for sharing, Donna!

Glitz, Glimmer and Lots of Shimmer:

Using Iridescent & Interference Fluid Acrylic Paints on Fabrics

There are two lines of Fluid Acrylics that can add shimmer, reflection, metallic touches and more to your fabric surfaces.

Iridescent Colors

These paints are largely made without actual color pigments and rely on mica particles with either reflective or refractive coatings to create the "color" that we perceive.

The gold, copper, silver, bronze, and pearl colors are known as Iridescent colors.

They leave a metallic-like glimmer on surfaces.

Interference Colors

The other line is known as Interference colors.

These act like the feathers on a hummingbird, throwing light around as the light hits the surface, or is refracted. This line of colors includes Violet, Red, Blue, Green, Gold, & Orange.

Each of these colors interacts beautifully with any other pigmented color you may choose to use, but especially well with the more sheer pigments in Fluid Acrylics (see list in Section on Acrylic Basics). You can shift your reds towards blue or your greens toward violet by adding a bit of interference to your mix.

I must warn you that they are somewhat addictive.

The great thing about using these colors on fabric is that you can transform colorful patterned fabric or create subtle pattern on colorful solid fabrics with very little effort.

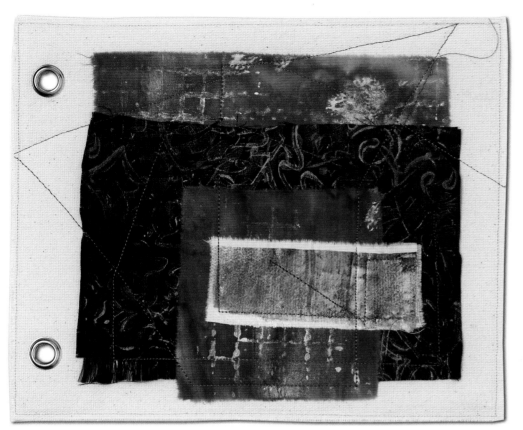

Fluid Acrylic Interference Paints...

The colors of the Fluid Interference paints are very subtle. When you see them in their containers you may be hard pressed to know that green is green or blue is blue, appearing more to be variations of whites.

To really see them at their most intense, paint a swatch over black fabric and see them come to life! The true nature of both the Iridescent and Interference colors really shows up after the paints are completely dry.

The mica particles are suspended in a clear medium which is white when it is wet. As it dries, it turns clear revealing the true beauty of these colors.

Border Marks

Make a few simple marks for a wonderful border. Apply the colors with stamps, a brush or a stencil.

Leaf Drawing

In this leaf drawing, the basic structure of the design was drawn on dry dark blue fabric using Iridescent Fluids and GAC 900 mixed together 1:1. Touches of Interference colors in the same ratio were introduced along the stem lines and for detail.

Large crescent areas of Interference/Fluid Color mixes that I painted on Steam-a-Seam were cut and applied according to the manufacturer's directions. (more on this process in the next section).

Final stitching details completed the design element. I've stitched down a number of my Iridescent/ Interference Fabric swatches so I will have a record of my experiments.

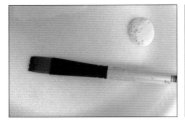

How to mix...

1. Squeeze out a few drops of your preferred Interference or Iridescent Fluid color onto a plate or palette (here I used Blue Interference). Squeeze out an equal amount of GAC 900. You will need a brush for mixing. 2. Pick up a small amount of Interference on your brush and work it into the bristles.

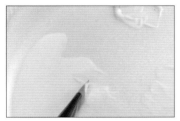

3. Dip your loaded brush into the GAC 900 and work that together on the plate. 4. Mix well before painting! You may apply the paint with a brush or sponge.

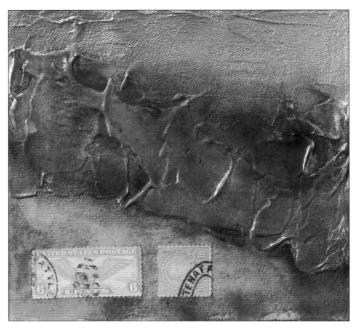

OPEN Medium mixed with Iridescent Gold Deep Fluid Acrylics

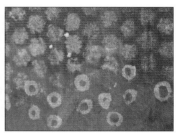
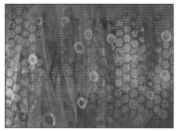

Iridescent & Interference Fluid Acrylics

Both of the first two fabrics were colorful and interesting in their own right, but didn't really meet my needs. A bit of stenciling through sequin waste and a few fine brush circles were added to make them camera ready. Interference paints, when applied in a sheer layer as a stenciled pattern, give off a shifting color as the fabric moves. Small additions of these specialty paints can really bring fabrics to life.

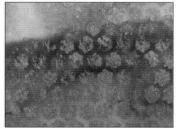
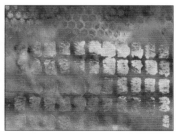

The close-up of the third swatch shows the difference between the Blue Interference and the Violet Interference when applied to the same piece of fabric.

The last swatch shows the addition of some Iridescent Fluid mixtures to the fabric surface. Notice how the Iridescent colors are somewhat more solid looking and truly reflect like metals.

TIP: When you add water to either of these two types of Fluid Paint, you release the mica particles from their polymer bond and they float out and migrate like a mist over the fabric, resulting in a soft sheen of sparkle. To prepare your fabric for this, just lightly mist it with water and apply the paints to the surface using a clean wet brush to drag the paint over the dampened fabric.

Just Add Paint

Fascinating Fusibles

I think of the Iridescent and Interference colors as jewelry for art. Their application can make even mundane things more interesting.

There a number of products on the market today that can be used in "out of the box" ways for much the same purpose. These products are known as fusibles. They are utilized in the sewing world for interfacings, appliqués, to bond two fabrics together, and much more.

Steam-a-Seam

Fusibles are comprised of various densities of a web-like substance that, when heated, melts and fuses two pieces together. They can be purchased as yardage or in pre-cut packages in most fabric departments. I have used Steam-A-Seam 2 (and Steam-A-Seam Lite) for its "traditional" purpose for years.

I especially like that it has a sticky back, allowing it to be repositioned until it is ironed down. The difference between the two is one of weight.

Mistyfuse

Another product known as Mistyfuse is a sheer web that is very lightweight and functions similarly to the other products, without adding any additional bulk. It is not repositionable.

I experimented with painting layers of fluid color (straight, not mixed with GAC 900) on each of these products. What a delight to see the web turn into iridescent gossamer wings and sparkling leaves, pods, and pomegranates.

At first I wasn't sure how much paint to use, how it would act once it was ironed, etc. But I was pleasantly surprised to learn that you could really get a range of looks out of one product just by controlling the amount of paint you applied, the direction or manner of strokes utilized (long and straight vs. short and patchy), or by leaving open spaces, or thinly painted areas amidst the more thickly painted areas.

This pod's shimmery blue sides are constructed of heavily painted pieces of Mistyfuse and embellished with zigzag stitching. You can see the individual fibers that make up the product. The color was made by mixing Interference Blue and Manganese Blue Hue together.

I used a flat brush to apply paint to the fusibles. Work on a craft mat with Mistyfuse as there is no paper backing. When working with the Steam-A-Seam products, just remove one layer of paper before painting, exposing the fusible surface.

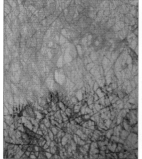 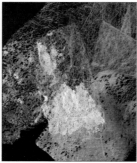  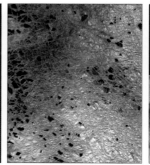 

Lightly-painted Mistyfuse. • Mistyfuse unpainted and painted in both thick and thin paint applications. • Steam-a-Seam Lite painted, with paper backing removed. This product has a circular pattern on it that creates an interesting interaction with lighter paint applications when it is ironed to fabric. • Here is a close-up of the painted Mistyfuse before I cut it into shapes. • I found it easiest to paint a number of pieces of the fusibles while I had my paints out and ready. I mixed colors and applied them here and there, overlapping and creating layers. This lets you have prepared material available for future projects without stopping and waiting for paint to dry. Mixing colors with the Interference and Iridescent Fluids into Fluid colors is so much fun!

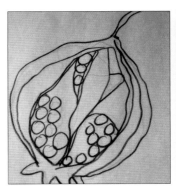 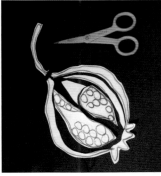  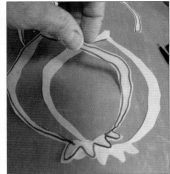

I Love Appliqué...

I have played with Applique for years both in fabric and on paper. It is a lot like fabric collage. Cutting and assembling, but instead of gluing, you stitch. By using the painted fusibles, you get to "glue" by ironing down your pieces in place and then stitch over them.

Here are the steps I took.

1. Start with a simple outline drawing right on the Steam-a-Seam cover paper.

2. Cut out the pieces. I did not cut out around the seeds. I wanted to paint details instead of having separate seeds.

3. Arrange your craft sheet, select your paints and layout the pieces of your drawing for reference.

4. Separate the top layer of paper from your drawing pieces and lay them aside for ready reference. Assemble the Steam-a-Seam parts on the craft sheet ready for painting.

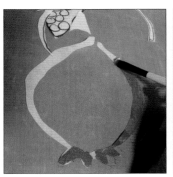 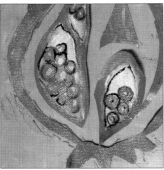 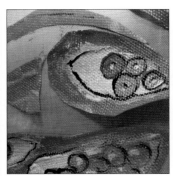 

5. Begin painting. I selected two reds (a cool Quinacridone Red, and a warmer Napthol Red in Fluid Paints, plus Red and Orange Interference Colors). I mixed them randomly together to get a lot of variations in my reds.

6. As I came to paint the seeds I realized I needed to add in a "white" so I chose the Iridescent Pearl Fluid and was able to use this white with the reds I had selected to create some pink areas. The final touches were done with Carbon Black Fluid Acrylic.

7. All the pieces must dry thoroughly before being ironed to fabric. The dots on the surface of the fusible are visible even after paint has been applied.

8. Once the paint is thoroughly dry, remove the backing papers from your fusible pieces.

 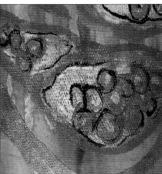 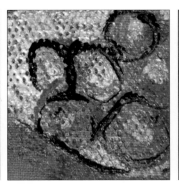 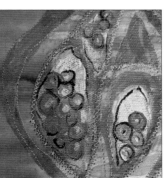

9. Reassemble the pieces on the fabric. You may wish to trim some pieces to adjust the spaces around the painted fusibles. I wanted more open space so I made minor snips here and there.

10. Follow the manufacturer's directions for fusing. It's important to wait until the fabric/fusible piece cools before removing your protective sheet. I used a Teflon craft sheet over my fabric while ironing.

11. A close-up of the fused pieces on my fabric of choice.

12. A close-up after I embellished with stitching on my machine. I found the surface a bit sticky, so I added a piece of transparent tracing paper on top and that made the stitching much easier.

Additional Applications...

Iron a piece of painted fusible to a coordinating piece of silk! You get extra shimmer for so little effort. Embellish it as you desire.

Print out your favorite images on Inkjet Printable Organza. Sandwich some painted fusible between your fabric base and the photo on organza. Fuse them together!

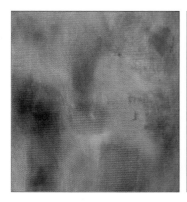

OPEN for Innovation:
A New Kind of Acrylic Paint
with All Kinds of Possibilities

Rarely does a truly new and innovative product come along! In 2008, Golden Artist Colors, after many years of research and development, released a unique line of Acrylic paints that have different properties from their traditional line of Fluid and Heavy Body Acrylics. These new paints are called OPEN Acrylics.

The qualities that set them apart have to do with the way they behave. Firstly they don't dry out rapidly like traditional acrylic paints, which means they work really well for techniques that take more time for preparation and set up. Because they don't dry out quickly you don't have to worry about ruining your brushes, brayers, stamps, or stencils by forgetting to wash the paint off right away.

The second wonderful thing about these paints is their creamy and smooth consistency. I have found them wonderful to blend, scrape, brayer, and paint with! Presently there are a limited number of colors out in the OPEN line, but more are on the way.

I feel confident that these remarkable new paints will find an important place in the mixed media artist's repertoire including the quilter and fiber artist.

Slower Drying Paints
for All Kinds of Ideas
and New Applications

Since all the OPEN products, including the OPEN Medium and OPEN Gel Gloss are fully compatible with other acrylic paints, it really makes purchasing a few colors and some of the OPEN Medium an affordable investment.

Try using the OPEN Medium with your Fluid Acrylics to create more working time, or combine the OPEN Paints with your Soft Gel for unique combinations and working properties.

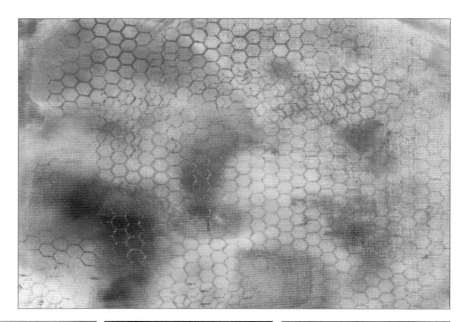

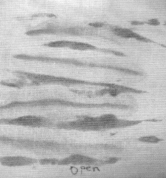

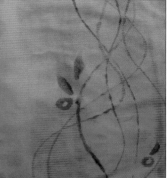

OPEN Acrylics diluted with water on antique coarse weave linen. Spritzed with water to encourage paint to move through fibers. It produced soft edges, no discernible change in hand and excellent color. Heat Set, washed & dried in the dryer.

OPEN acrylics on antique coarse weave linen applied with a wet brush on dry fabric. The paint bled only into the areas of wetness created by the strokes from the brush.

OPEN acrylics (blue lines) added to a traditionally dyed piece of fabric. Paint was thinned with water before application. No discernable change in hand between original fabric after dyeing and fabric after paint was added.

Patt Blair created this piece of fabric using OPEN and water. If you look back to page 10, you can see it after she quilted it. The striations are an example of how beautifully you can create blends with two colors using the OPEN Acrylics.

What I discovered during the writing of this book was that there was an immediate attraction between OPEN and fabrics.

It was love at first contact! OPEN made silk-screening, stamping, mono-printing, block printing, & deconstructed screen-printing effortless. It loved being turned into soft washes for a water-color effect. It responded with enthusiasm to every task I put before it.

And finally…it is completely washable both machine washable & dryable, ironable, and stitchable! By far the techniques I tried with OPEN gave me some of the best outcomes in "hand" out of all the acrylic techniques in this book.

Anytime you introduce a little water to the OPEN paints they just relax into the fibers.

Remember that you need to allow the OPEN Paints to DRY COMPLETELY before you launder them. If there is any tack left to the surface, continue to allow the paint to cure.

This will take longer than when you use traditional acrylic paints and depends on how thickly you apply the layers. Thinner or wetter layers will dry more quickly than layers of straight OPEN.

To create sheer colors or transparent glazes, add OPEN Medium to the paint. Adding water flattens the paint down and carries pigments into the fibers, almost like dye.

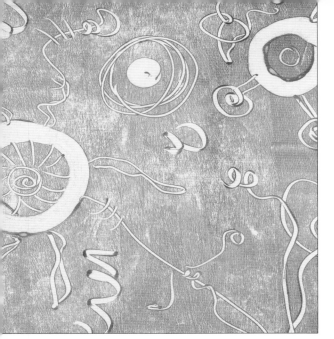

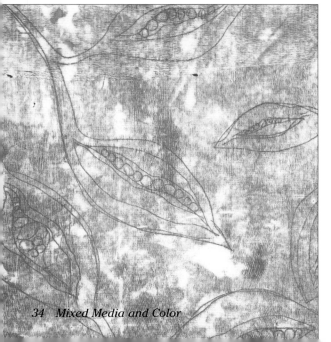

Monoprints with OPEN
"Mono (one) + Print =
Creating a Single Print of an Image"

Monoprinting is the easiest way to create a print. Using OPEN paints, with their ability to stay wet longer and blend so easily, makes the process of printmaking a snap for beginners and experienced artists alike.

To make a monoprint you will need a flat smooth surface. I use a piece of glass or Plexiglas. To protect myself from cuts while handling the glass, I wrap the edges with metal tape. I prefer a clear surface because sometimes I place images under the surface to help me draw.

In addition you will need a rubber brayer (not a sponge brayer or paint roller), some OPEN paint, a palette knife, a small paintbrush and something to make fine lines (toothpicks, chopsticks, or paint shapers work great). Let's get started.

1. Squeeze out a small amount of 2 or three colors onto your glass surface. I used Quinacridone Magenta, Indian Yellow Hue and Hansa Yellow Medium. Scrape it onto your plate with your palette knife. It's OK if the colors touch each other.

2. With the brayer, roll out the colors over the entire glass surface; mix them together as you go. You will feel the paint begin to get sticky as you roll back and forth with the brayer. This is good. You are ready to make some marks. Notice how you can actually see through to the darker colors that are sitting on the plate. You will see how this comes into play.

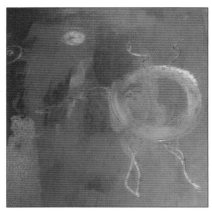 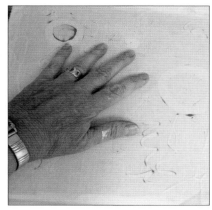

3. Using your paintbrush and other tools, draw into the surface of the paint layer on the glass plate. After each stroke, wipe the paint off of your brush or tip so that you don't end up putting it back on the plate with your next stroke! I created a wide circle using a flat tip brush and the smaller lines were made with a rubber tipped paint shaper tool.

4. Gently lay your fabric or paper over the entire painted surface. Smooth down with the palm of your hand. You should begin to see the image transferring to the fabric almost immediately. Be sure that all the fabric is touching the painted plate. Lift the fabric off the plate and let it dry thoroughly.

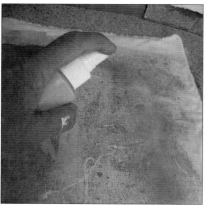
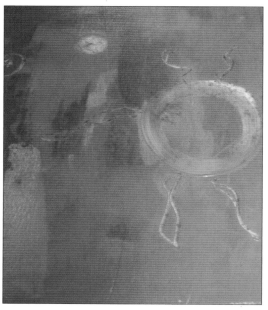

For fun, you can lift the ghost print left on the plate. Spritz the plate with water, place and smooth down another piece of fabric, spritzing it as well.

When you lift you will see a softer, more watery version of the original mono-print. Two for the work of one!

Monoprints - Take 2

I mentioned that I like to work on a clear surface when I monoprint. Here is why. I teach a lot of classes where students are anxious about drawing things. I create simple line drawings that help them to move forward. I like to place these simple line drawings under the plate to use as a guide for creating a different kind of monoprint.

1. Here is a simplified drawing of a pomegranate placed under a glass plate. Note the metal tape that has been applied to the edges of the glass to protect from cuts. Center the drawing under the plate.

2. Select some appropriate colors of OPEN Acrylics and paint onto the glass surface letting the drawing keep your image on track. I chose two colors of red as I wanted to blend them for a more interesting surface.

3. After you have placed all of your main body of color (red in this case) take a tool (I'm using a paint shaper with a rubber tip). Draw the lines back into the surface of the painted area on the plate. This will give your monoprint a lot more dimension.

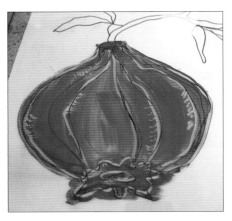

4. Add in the remainder of the color details and line to finish

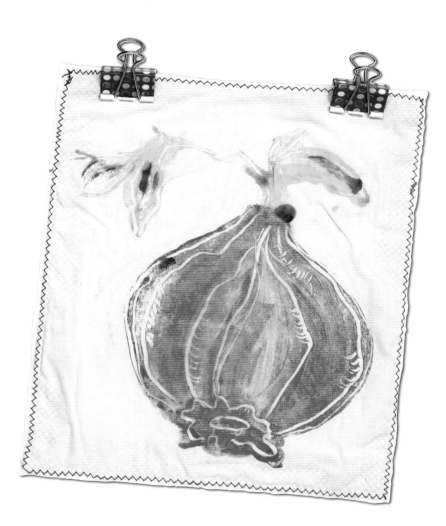

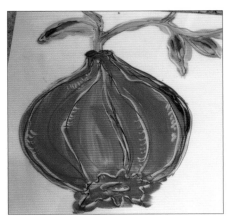

5. The rest of the process is the same as in the prior technique, place your fabric, smooth, and lift.

The Pomegranate on polka dot piece: I chose to cut the white areas out of my monoprint and place the remaining image over red and white dotted fabric to mimic the pomegranate seeds.

I used a zigzag stitch to sew it down. I was able to lift a ghost print off the plate and used it for the backing.

The green lines on this monoprint were created using this technique.

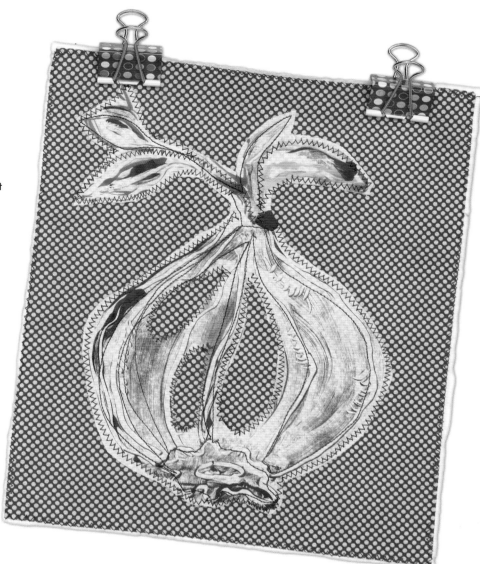

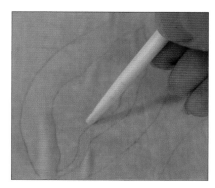

Lay down your blank fabric FIRST! Yes, first.

Now be brave and take a pointed tool or chopstick and gently draw onto the back of your fabric. Keep it simple at first. You could trace an image onto paper and then place that paper on top of your cloth to use as a guide if you are too timid to freehand it!

Just give it a shot!

Monoprints - Take 3:

Begin by selecting your paint colors. Use the brayer to create a smooth even coat of paint on your glass plate. Here is where it differs from the prior monoprinting techniques we have tried:

Variation:
Try double monoprints!

After your first print is dry, use a different color, make a different design and print over your first one!

By the way, all of these techniques result in very little change to the hand of the fabrics that I used.

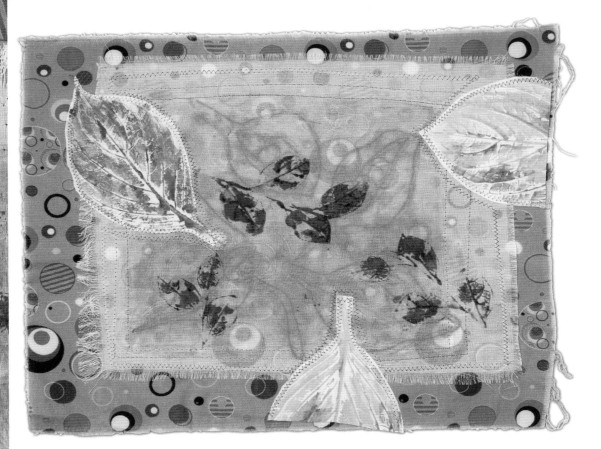

Opening up to Nature

I love my garden and since my studio is in the garden I am gloriously aware of the nuances of the many leaves, branches, and blossoms that are within my view. There is a wonderful hydrangea plant just outside my studio door that has honored me with magnificent blooms for the entire summer. I plucked a leaf from it to try this next experiment. I think you will be happy with the results.

Nature prints have been around for a long time. Inking, rolling & pounding techniques abound, but now with only a few strokes of OPEN Acrylics mixed with a little OPEN Medium, you can make fabulous prints from your favorite plant forms in minutes.

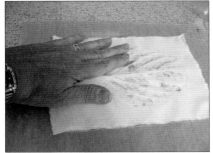

1. These are the leaves I selected, rinsed and dried. Then I placed them face down on my craft sheet awaiting paint. It is better to print the back of the leaves for a more realistic impression.

2. Mix a small amount of OPEN Medium in with your OPEN color of choice. I started with Naples Yellow Hue. Brush onto the back of a leaf. I added additional colors such as Green Gold, Sap Green Hue, and Alizarin Crimson Hue as well for a more natural variation.

3. Place fabric over leaf, smooth and press into the grooves of the leaf; you will see the image coming through. I recommend using lightweight papers such as rice paper as an alternative to fabric.

4. For my branch with multiple leaves I selected Quinacridone Magenta, Dioxazine Purple and Green Gold OPEN Acrylics mixing each with a small amount of OPEN Medium.

I painted the magenta and purple areas first, liberally mixing them to create some mid-tones. At the end I dabbed on a tiny bit of Green Gold.

5. As before, lay the fabric over the painted leaves and press gently with fingers to insure good contact with the paint.

6. Lift fabric to reveal print. Continue pressing painted branch onto fabric to get more prints. Each will be a little less intense than the one before.

Block Printing
Techniques with OPEN Acrylics

I mentioned earlier in the book that I have many rubber stamps. In the last few years I have begun to cut larger "stamps" or blocks using a soft eraser type material and a few simple tools.

I began with 1½" blocks onto which I cut simple designs and it just progressed from there. It took me awhile to really get the hang of what to remove and what to leave on the blocks, but it was well worth the learning process. In recent months I've cut larger blocks which are great for working on fabric. I still use my little blocks for developing and filling in patterns. They are my "bag of tricks" for creating pattern, so to speak.

The Mastercarve Tool Set I use is made by Staedtler. While Staedtler makes the carving blocks, several other companies make similar products and they seem to all work well and are equally easy to carve into. There are lots of books out there that are guides to cutting blocks or stamps, so I'll encourage you to explore this process on your own.

The reason I include it here is that the OPEN paints work so well for pulling complex prints off these easy to carve blocks. Feel free to carve as much detail into your block as you desire!

When you work with fabric, you are using a flexible receiver for your print. This allows you to assist the process by pressing the fabric into the areas of detail you have cut into the block. When doing this process with paper it is important to burnish the surface of the paper adequately to insure good contact and an ideal print.

Hint: Using a burnishing tool or batten assists that process even more; even a wooden spoon will work.

The blocks are easily washed and can be used over and again.

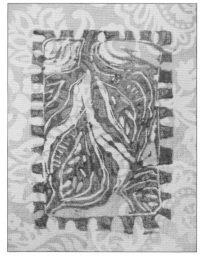

By varying the colors you ink your block with, you can create a series of one-of-a-kind prints.

Try using patterned fabric, the back of patterned fabric, dyed, painted or colorized fabric silks, cotton, or sheers. This process lends itself well to quilters who wish to utilize a repetitive image but still have variety of color and texture.

The central image of the bird in the tree on this piece, which was quilted and finished by Patt Blair, is a large hand-cut block that I cut. You will see it in pieces throughout this book. It is a favorite of mine. The same image can appear quite different when utilized on various fabrics or when printed in other colors. Try using both dry and wet fabrics.

Another Door
COLLAGRAPH PRINTS

A Collagraph is simply a print made from materials that are glued or affixed to a rigid surface... sort of like a 'collage' of items made into a printing plate. These materials are then inked (in our case we will use OPEN Acrylics for our color) and a print is lifted from the surface. I have created a very simple Collagraph to share the process.

 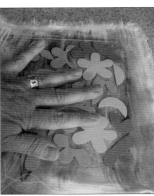 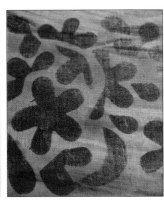 

Affix the foam pieces to the Plexiglas piece in a suitable arrangement. Cut Foam pieces to fit if needed or to create interest.

1. Use a brayer to roll out a small amount of OPEN Acrylic on a craft sheet fully inking the brayer. Roll the brayer over the foam pieces. Repeat to insure that the paint has transferred from the brayer to the collagraph plate.

2. Select your fabric or paper and place the collagraph plate paint side down onto the fabric surface and use your hand to press the plate firmly onto the cloth. It is a good idea to have a bit of padding under the fabric.

3. Lift the plate and reveal the print.

4. Re-ink the collagraph plate and use it on a different fabric or paper.

I started with a 5x7 piece of Plexiglas and some pre-cut shapes made out of self-stick craft foam. These are readily available in many craft stores and are easy to cut and stick firmly onto the Plexiglas. Whole sheets are also available if you want to create more complex collagraph plates. You may also make them out of cardboard and other found objects.

I find that a coat of Gesso plus two coats of Polymer Medium protects the cardboard collagraph plates allowing for easier change of colors and multiple uses.

Completed collagraph print on white cotton fabric.

This is a more complex collagraph plate.
1. Make the plate with cardboard and mesh pieces, glued to cardboard. Coat it with gesso and two coats of Fluid Polymer Medium.
2. Place fabric over the inked collagraph plate. Spritz with water.
3. Expose the print.
4. Add details with a fine brush using colors of straight OPEN Acrylics on the back side of print. The colors will seep through to the front of the fabric and give a soft look.

Resists are simple barriers to color. They can be created in a variety of ways. In this image of the tree, the barrier is first created by stitching a line drawing.

This defined the positive and negative areas and helped me determine where to place the paint. I then painted the entire piece with layers of Quinacridone Magenta and Transparent Pyrrole Orange Fluid Acrylics diluted with water.

When this was dry I over-painted the interior shapes with Interference Acrylic and added detail with other colors.

Creating Resists

Resists are simply barriers. They can be created in a variety of ways.

Polymer Medium is an ideal product to do just that! It is fluid enough that you can apply it through a very fine tip to create beautiful drawings that will resist the colorizing techniques we discussed earlier in the book, yet it is viscous enough to stay in place while it dries.

1. I created a very simple example by drawing a spiral form on a piece of white cotton muslin fabric with the Medium which is white when it is wet and clear when it is dry. It comes with a built in signal to let you know when it is ready!

2. To colorize the white fabric and bring the resist pattern into play, create a colorizing mix using the airbrush paint and GAC 900 formula we discussed earlier in the book.

3. Place the fabric into a bath of the color mixture of your choice, I chose blue.

4. Remove after 5-10 minutes, squeeze, and allow to air dry. Heat set using a Teflon craft sheet.

The spiral pattern really pops off the page with the addition of the color.

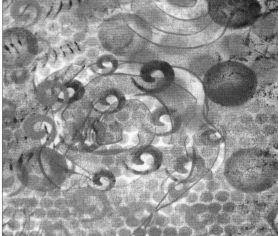

Using Shiva Paintstiks

Enhancing fabric design with Shiva Paintstiks is not a new idea. I was curious to see how they would react when applied over fabrics painted or printed with Acrylic mixtures. I was very pleased with the outcome. Give it a try.

Shiva Paintstiks were used with a stencil to add detail and leaves to this printed fabric

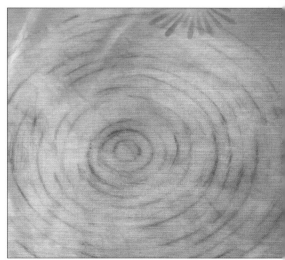

Photo 1 - Shiva paintsticks were applied with a foam applicator through a stencil over an acrylic monoprint on fabric.

Photo 2 - Paintstiks added the leaves to this double monoprinted tree.

Photo 3 - Shiva Paintstik were used over a texture plate and through stencils to create the concentric circles on this Acrylic "tie-dye" piece.

Photo 4 - The fabric was colorized with Acrylic, Paintstiks were used to embellish the surface, and the fabric was torn in half. One half was given a second color bath. The Paintstiks acted as a resist and remained distinct!

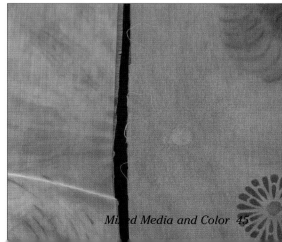

Images and fabrics that relate to a specific colorway are sewn together in a block.

Pretty Images
from Inkjet Printable Photo Fabrics

I'll admit it had been a long time since I had purchased prepackaged fabrics that were designed to go through my Inkjet printer. I think the last time I bought something it was a "decal" process that let you iron on an image. I have been seriously out of touch with what's available in the market. I bought a number of packets of different fabrics from several companies in an effort to examine their outcomes and determine their color, stability and their washability. Although pricey, this was a good decision several reasons.

It turns out that there is considerable range of color quality and intensity. Some of the brands did an outstanding job of producing the photo image on the fabric as if it were on high quality photo paper. Others, well, let's just say there was room for improvement.

The images I printed on all of the products I tried were waterproof after following simple instructions. The instructions varied a bit, but essentially were soaking or rinsing in cold water, air dry, heat set, etc.

I had two definite favorites: EQ Printables and June Tailor Colorfast.

WOW! The images were sharp, bright, and gorgeous. The EQ fabric was of a much lighter weight than the June Tailor Colorfast, so for some people that may be a factor.

I encourage people to do their own tests as each Inkjet printer company has its own ink formulas which certainly influence the outcomes. I have a Canon photo quality printer so my outcomes are based solely on that machine.

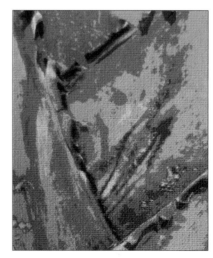

This is a close-up of an image I took with my camera, altered in Photoshop, and then printed on my inkjet printer. Note the good color and detail. You can see all of the areas of color quite clearly.

Simple Process

The process is very easy and the packages of Inkjet Printable Photo Fabrics come with a set of printed instructions.

The real fun comes in selecting the images and deciding how to utilize them. I will share a few of my ideas.

Several images of radishes The variations were quite dramatic... using the same printer but printed on different Printable Fabrics

Elephant and green silk

Digital photo, manipulated in Photoshop, then printed on cotton and again on organza combined with other fabrics with stitch embellishments.

I manipulated this photo of a Rabbit in Photoshop, then printed it on cotton, then stitched it to fabric pieces.

Beehive banner

Comparison between white pre-coated fabrics and Digital Grounds coated green fabrics with the same images.

Digital Mixed Media
Products on Fabrics

There have been many advances in the world of digital art over the last couple of decades. Almost everyone has a digital camera, hundreds of images stored on their computer and never enough time to print them. Golden Artist Colors released a line of surface coatings called Digital Grounds in 2008. These liquid formulations are meant to coat various surfaces, including fabric, allowing the surfaces to receive inkjet inks with ease and clarity. For fabrics the Digital Grounds Clear or the Digital Grounds White, which have been formulated for absorbent surfaces, are recommended. Should you wish to print on a plasticized or vinyl fabric, then you would need to use the Digital Grounds Clear for Non-absorbent surfaces.

How do you choose between the Digital Grounds Clear and the White? Think of what you are printing and how much the image will compliment or compete with the fabric. If the fabric is a busy print that will visually fight with your image, you can use the Digital Grounds White to tone down the surface of the fabric. It's a bit like gesso in this regard. It goes on kind of milky but dries white. After the requisite two coats are added, the busyness of the existing pattern will be much more subdued. I chose to use this product over some bright green painted fabric to show you how well it covers.

Whenever you wish total visibility of the fabric through the image you are printing, use the Digital Grounds Clear.

Digital Grounds

There is one important difference between the fabrics prepared using the Digital Grounds and the packages of white fabrics sold for photo printing. The fabrics prepared and printed using Digital Grounds are NOT washable. These products are water-soluble by design. The water-based ink needs a water receptive surface to enable it to print properly. There is an advantage to these fabrics that pre-packaged printable can't offer as well - with the Digital Grounds you can choose any color, any pattern, any kind of fabric that will fit through your printer. You are not limited to printing on white fabric.

To give some protection (both UV and against water damage) to your printed fabrics use two light coats of Golden's Archival Aerosol MSA Varnish with UVLS. Follow safety precautions when utilizing this product.

Flower on fabric colored with airbrush paints

  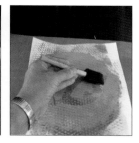

Photo 1 - The application process is very easy. Since you will be feeding the fabric through your ink-jet printer, I recommend ironing your fabrics of choice to freezer paper. This will provide the fabric with stability. I like the pre-cut packs of 50 heavyweight pieces of freezer paper by C. Jenkins that sold through Dharma Trading Company.

Photo 2 - Once you have your fabric ironed to the freezer paper and trimmed to fit through your printer, you will need to apply two coats of the Digital Grounds that you have selected on the fabric.

Photo 3 - The first coat is applied with all strokes going in a horizontal direction. When the first coat is dry, then apply a second coat with strokes going in a vertical direction. I prefer to use an inexpensive foam brush for this process. You need only wash it out in sudsy water to reuse it.

Photo 4 - Once your fabrics are prepared, you may select your photos, alter them or not, and print them out. • Photo 5 - Final photo printed over the green fabric with Digital Grounds White. • Photo 6 - Black & White image printed on multi-colored screen-printed fabric with Digital Grounds Clear.

Water lily piece

Fusions
Mixed Media Applications

Fusions are sort of like expanded collages. Pieces which combine Fibers, Fabrics, Papers, Images and Acrylics. They are stitchable surfaces that have texture, interest, and a joie de vivre.

These wonderful collage pieces are changeable over the course of their construction and can be joined together, expanded, or modified at any point during their construction or even after you are done!

Just add more paint or more elements, cut, stitch, or glue! It's up to you.

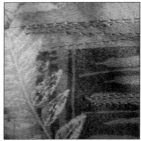

Other Fusion Ideas...

Photo 1 - Add a photo printed on inkjet ready fabrics, a few decorative stitches, ribbon, yarn and you are ready to go! • Photo 2 - Stamping, block printing, drawing, painting, sewing...my kind of art. • Photo 3 - Close-up of stitching used to create line and form. Use more than one color and some metallics for effect.

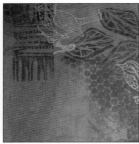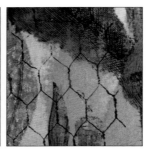

Photo 4 - Iridescent and Interference Fluids with GAC 900 over airbrush painted fabric, stitched for embellishment. • Photo 5 - Playful stamped images of birds on a complex background. • Photo 6 - Paints, stamps, texture blocks, & transfers.

Fushion of a face printed on
dyed tan fabric and then collaged

Fusions refer to techniques that combine Fibers and Paints with something more such as Paper and Mediums (primarily Soft Gel, Polymer Medium, or Fluid Matte Medium) to create semi-flexible yet stitchable mixed-media pieces.

In a Fusion you create a base out of paper, fabric, and other notions in which numerous layers are then fused together with an Acrylic Medium. This base can be painted, sewn and embellished as you wish.